COFFEE

OUR DAILY
CUP

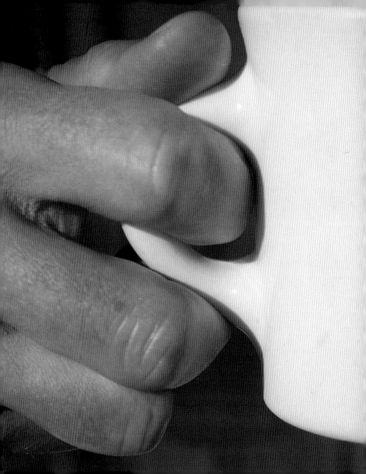

They have in Turkey a drink called coffee, made of a berry of the same name, as black as soot, and of a strong scent, but not aromatical; which they take, beaten into powder, in water, as hot as they can drink it; and they take it, and sit at it in their coffee houses, which are like our taverns. The drink comforteth the brain and heart, and helpeth digestion.

—Sir Francis Bacon

COFFEE

OUR DAILY
CUP

Suzanne Kotz and Ed Marquand

Warner 🅦 Treasures™

Published by Warner Books
A Time Warner Company

Warner Treasures is a trademark of Warner Books, Inc.
1271 Avenue of the Americas
New York, NY 10020

 A Time Warner Company

Text by *Suzanne Kotz*
Book design and photography by Ed Marquand

Printed in Hong Kong
First Printing: March 1996
10 9 8 7 6 5 4 3 2 1

ISBN: 0-446-91138-0

CONTENTS

AH, COFFEE

No beverage can compare with coffee in the social and companionable qualities it imparts. Tea has always been a soft, soothing drink for gentle women and men of mild power and peaceful walks. Coffee, on the other hand, has ever been associated with the robust, the daring, and the adventurous—including the man who first served the brew to Parisians.

In 1672 an Armenian named Pascal came from Constantinople to Paris and opened the city's first coffeehouse. Prior to his appearance, the beverages sold in Parisian restaurants were home-brewed beer, apple and pear cider, honey-and-water, milk, and wine. But Pascal sold only coffee, and his audacity attracted curious customers while throwing his competitors into a green rage. Pascal made a fortune, and for years nobody dreamed that coffee could be made by anyone but the visitor from Turkey.

In 1686, however, a Sicilian, Francesco Procopio dei Coltelli, opened a café across the street from the Comédie Française. He did a reasonable trade in spices, ices, barley water, lemonade, and milk, but when he added coffee to the menu, the political and literary elite of the city turned out in droves. Paris's infatuation with coffee had just begun; by the end of the eighteenth century, some seven hundred cafés had sprung up, and by the mid-nineteenth century, Parisians could pick from as many as three thousand coffeehouses.

American coffee drinkers may not have as many cafés to choose from, but they have discovered the coffee craze. Excellent coffee is now readily available from an increasing number of commercial purveyors, and never has there been such a wide choice of beans, roasts, grinds, and brewing methods. This guide will help you decide what you like and will teach you how to make cup after cup of great coffee at home.

THE COFFEE
BEAN

COFFEE BEANS

The coffee plant (family Rubiacaeae, genus *Coffea*) is native only to Africa and Yemen; from these countries its cultivation spread to other regions of the world. Two coffee species are commercially grown: *Coffea arabica* and *Coffea robusta*. *Arabica,* accounting for 80 percent of the world's coffee production, is used in specialty coffees. *Robusta* finds its way into cheaper blends and is the basis of instant coffee.

Coffee beans are actually the seeds of ripe coffee "cherries." Because the fruit of the coffee plant does not ripen uniformly—flowering branches, green fruit, and ripe berries occur all together—coffee cherries are still hand-picked. To get to the coffee bean, processors must wash or dry the fruit. Either method separates the green coffee bean from its pulp and skin.

The flavor and aroma of coffee beans, like wine grapes, are determined by the growing conditions and methods of the area of the world in which they are produced. Colombian coffee is the most familiar varietal grown in Central and South America. Coffees from this region are medium-bodied with a clean, elegant flavor. From the East African countries of Ethiopia and Kenya come full-bodied coffees with an intense, rich character. Some say these beans have an almost floral quality. The rarest varietal, Arabian Mocha, is from Yemen and is an integral part of the classic blend, Mocha Java. Pacific Rim countries produce full-flavored, smooth coffees with a spicy, earthy taste.

Coffee roasters make their own blends that high-light the distinctive characteristics of each varietal. The labeling of blends and varietals, however, is woefully inconsistent. The hapless buyer is confronted by a welter of names—Colombian Supremo, Mocha Java, Guatemalan Antigua—and a variety of roasts—Italian, French, Espresso, Full-City. These designations, which the consumer can use only as general guides, are wholly at the discretion of the seller. Be aware that the name under which beans are sold does not necessarily mean that the coffee is a pure varietal, or even blended from the beans identified in the label.

The confusion extends to coffee drinks as well. "Mocha Java," for example, has become a generic term for a chocolate-flavored coffee, but more

correctly refers to a blend of two specific varietals—Arabian Mocha and Indonesian Java. Mocha is a small city in Yemen, located at the tip of the Arabian peninsula on the Red Sea. Coffee grown on its nearby hillsides was first exported to Europe four centuries ago. Today the amount of coffee exported from Yemen is very small, but aficionados treasure the bean's complex character and heavy body. "Java" properly refers to beans of *Coffea arabica* grown on the island of Java (some will accept beans grown anywhere in Indonesia in this definition). Genuine "Mocha Java" is a blend of beans from Yemen and Java.

COFFEE ROASTING

All coffee beans are roasted to bring out their intrinsic quality and flavor. Like a vintner blending grapes, the roaster decides which characteristics to emphasize or mute by adjusting the duration and heat of the roast, and by continually judging the color and aroma of the beans.

During the roasting process, water in the bean dissipates, and it begins to darken. A series of chemical reactions transforms the starches and sugars into the oils that give coffee much of its aroma and flavor. The longer beans are roasted, the more of these aromatic oils move toward the surface.

Contrary to popular thinking, you can't judge the quality of a bean by its color. In darker roasts, the flavor of the bean is overtaken by the degree of the roast; what you taste is the smoky "burnt" flavor imparted by the roast. And the "strength" of a cup of coffee has nothing to do with the roast itself; it depends on the proportion of water to coffee used in brewing. Dark-roasting itself doesn't produce stronger coffee.

ROAST CHART

✤ CINNAMON (OR HALF-CITY) ROAST ✤

pale brown; canned coffee

✤ CITY ROAST ✤

light brown; acidity outweighs sweetness

✤ FULL-CITY ROAST ✤

chestnut brown; a careful balance of
acid to sugar

✤ ESPRESSO ROAST ✤

chocolate brown; acid taste diminished

✤ ITALIAN ROAST ✤

dark chocolate; sweet, tangy flavor

✤ FRENCH ROAST ✤

nearly black; pungent, smoky taste

BLENDS

The goal of a coffee blend is to combine in one cup the most pleasing traits of various coffees. Knowledgeable of the particular qualities of different beans, the master blender skillfully balances the characteristics of each: a flavorful but light bean, for example, might be rounded out by the addition of a more full-bodied bean. Variable growing and harvesting conditions mean that the components of coffee blends change over time. A specialty blender must constantly fine-tune his or her blend to maintain a consistent flavor.

If you buy beans from a specialty shop, you can try your own hand at blending. Select a well-balanced coffee as a foundation, to which you add another bean whose flavor or body you enjoy. Or try a combination of light and dark roasts of the same bean.

DECAF

If you want the rich flavor of coffee without the jolt of caffeine, try decaffeinated beans. Once made only from inferior beans, decaf now comes in as many premium varietals as regular coffee.

Decaf beans typically are treated with a penetrating chemical solvent. When the solvent is drained, about 98 percent of the caffeine goes with it. Another method, the Swiss Water process, decaffeinates beans without chemicals. Some find the flavor of water-processed beans to be less satisfying, but beans decaffeinated this way are increasingly available in specialty stores.

And what happens to the caffeine? Most of it is sold to drug manufacturers and soft drink companies.

STORAGE

Coffee beans begin to lose their flavor within weeks of roasting, and grinding accelerates flavor loss even further. Store your coffee in an airtight container; exposure to air causes oils containing aroma and flavor to evaporate. And because grinding exposes more of the bean's surface to air, grind your beans at home, just before brewing. Ground coffee keeps for seven to ten days, but whole beans last up to three times longer.

Should you refrigerate or freeze your beans? Some say that refrigeration retards deterioration; others say that moisture (another flavor enemy) condenses on the beans every time you open your chilled container, outweighing the benefit. The best solution is to buy only a week's supply of beans at a time.

STORAGE RECOMMENDATIONS

1

Grind only what you need.

2

Keep beans in an airtight container at room temperature.

3

If you are holding beans for long-term storage, freeze them in an airtight, moisture-proof container. Glass is the preferred container because it won't retain unwanted flavors. Beans can be ground right from the freezer; no thawing is necessary.

GRINDING

Grind your beans at home and your coffee will benefit from the extra flavor retained by the whole bean. And there is nothing quite like the aroma of freshly ground beans. A good blade grinder is not very expensive. By simply varying the grinding time, you can produce a coarse or fine grind.

GRINDING TIMES

COARSE (French press) 6 to 8 seconds

MEDIUM (flat filters/drip) 10 seconds

FINE (vacuum/Neapolitan flip) 20 seconds

EXTRA FINE (cone filters/steam espresso)
25 seconds

VERY FINE (pump or piston espresso machines)
35 seconds

BREWING

COFFEE BREWING ESSENTIALS

Make sure your equipment is clean

Oils accumulate every time you brew and can make subsequent cups bitter. Soak filter holders and coffee baskets occasionally in a 5:1 water-and-vinegar solution to remove residue. Rinse thoroughly with hot water.

Use good water

Coffee is almost all water, and if your tap water doesn't taste fresh, your coffee won't either. Use filtered or bottled water for the best flavor, but avoid distilled water—it is flat and tasteless.

Measure carefully

The standard coffee measure is two level tablespoons to six ounces of water. Remember that coffee doesn't stretch—amounts of coffee and water should be carefully balanced to the brewing method you are using.

Don't boil your coffee

Hot water draws out the flavor of the bean, but water at a hard boil will cook your coffee. Use water that is just below the boiling point. And always start with freshly drawn cold water—hot water can be flat and stale.

Serve it fresh

Coffee's flavor begins to deteriorate within fifteen minutes of brewing, so don't leave your pot on the back burner! Brew just before serving, and use a vacuum thermos to keep the coffee warm.

BREWING METHODS
Direct drip

Direct drip brewing is easy and convenient. Electric drip machines are plentiful, but manually preparing a cup or a pot takes almost no time, and the resulting coffee has a fresher taste. Any drip filtering method uses the same basic equipment: a paper (or fine wire mesh) filter, a cone to hold the filter, and a pot or cup into which the coffee drips.

To prepare, measure finely ground coffee into the filter fitted into the cone. Slowly pour hot water over the ground coffee, gradually topping it off as the water passes through the filter.

Automatic drip

The electric percolator, invented more than a century after the development of drip pots, was a sad step backward in coffee making. Thankfully, it has been replaced on most kitchen and office counters with an automatic drip coffeemaker. Nearly all these devices rely on a paper filter and produce excellent coffee if served fresh. But beware the pot that sits on the warming plate for hours!

Most models follow the same convenient and functional design. You simply measure coffee into the filter basket, pour cold water into the heating tank, and turn on the switch.

Plunger

The plunger, or French press, has the advantage of style: its glass-and-metal 1920s design makes it attractive in any setting.

Warm the glass beaker by rinsing it with hot water. Measure coarsely ground coffee into the beaker, add hot water, stir briefly, replace the plunger (but do not depress), and allow the brew to steep for three to four minutes. Then slowly push the plunger down, forcing the grounds to the bottom of the beaker.

Vacuum pot

The glass-globed vacuum pot is undoubtedly the most dramatic coffee brewing system around. Stove-top versions are available as well as a more elegant tabletop brewer with a spirit lamp for heat. Using a vacuum pot is tricky—its glass parts are fragile and difficult to handle when hot—but once mastered, it produces excellent coffee.

To make coffee, measure coarsely ground granules into the top globe and cold water into the bottom. As the water heats, steam pressure forces it into the top chamber, where it mixes with the ground coffee. Give the grounds a stir, remove the pot from the heat (or extinguish the flame), and in a minute or two the liquid is drawn back into the lower pot, leaving the grounds behind.

Thermal carafe

One of the simplest brewing methods uses a filter cone specially fitted for an insulated thermal carafe. Coffee drips directly into the thermos, which protects the coffee's full flavor and aroma without any threat of overcooking. The thermos will be more effective if you briefly rinse its chamber with hot water before using. Even if you don't brew coffee into a thermos, consider using one to keep your coffee hot and tasting fresh.

ESPRESSO

Espresso, contrary to popular opinion, is neither a bean nor a roast, but a brewing method. The sign of a truly perfect espresso is *crema,* a creamy golden layer floating on the surface. Espresso can be made in a stove-top pot or with a countertop espresso machine.

The stove-top pot has two chambers, between which rests a filter. To use, fill the base of the pot with cold water. Measure finely ground coffee into the filter, and place it back into the base. Be sure to pack the grounds carefully. If too tight, water cannot penetrate; if too loose, the brew will be too weak. Screw the top onto the base and place the pot over medium heat. Pressure will force the water up through the grounds. When all the water has passed through the grounds, you will hear a gurgling sound —your coffee is ready.

Countertop machines operate on the same basic principle: pressurized hot water is forced through a filter holding finely ground coffee. Operation varies from machine to machine: some work with the touch of a button, others operate with a spring-powered piston handle. Follow the instructions provided by the manufacturer. Most countertop machines come with a nozzle for steaming milk, allowing you to make caffè latte and cappuccino at home.

ESPRESSO LEXICON

✤ *Espresso:* the essence of fine coffee, extracted under pressure. Intense and aromatic, a cup, or "shot," of espresso contains about the same amount of coffee as a regular cup, but with far less water—about 1½ ounces.

✤ *Espresso ristretto:* a regular espresso but short, or "restricted," to just under 1 ounce.

✤ *Espresso Americano:* also called "espresso lungo," a single shot diluted with hot water to produce a milder or "long" espresso.

✤ *Espresso doppio:* a double serving, or two shots.

✤ *Espresso macchiato:* espresso "stained" with a tablespoon or two of frothed milk.

✤ *Latte macchiato:* steamed milk "stained" with a shot of espresso.

✤ *Cappuccino:* espresso with steamed milk, topped by a head of foamed milk, in roughly equal portions. The name comes from the "cap" of foam, which Italians thought resembled the hooded robe worn by Capuchin monks.

✤ *Caffè latte:* a single serving of espresso and hot steamed milk, with just the barest foam head.

✤ *Caffè mocha:* roughly equal parts espresso, chocolate syrup, and steamed milk, usually topped by whipped cream.

✤ *Espresso con panna:* espresso topped by a dollop of whipped cream.

CONTINENTAL
COFFEE

Some coffee consumers are bewildered by the order-
ing of American espresso, which ostensibly occurs
in English. You might think that once you've
mastered the terminology you'll be home free in a
Parisian café or an Italian coffee bar. And you will
be—almost. A few key distinctions and additional
phrases will help.

In France, if you order a *café noir,* you won't get
black American coffee, but a single shot of espresso.
Order a *café filtre* if you are looking for American-
style coffee. For extra-strong espresso, ask for a *café
serré;* for a weak espresso, try a *café allongé,* which

often comes with a beaker of hot water so customers can dilute the coffee to their own taste.

In Italy, *caffè* will get you an espresso; the closest thing to American filtered coffee is an *espresso lungo,* a shot of espresso with twice the water. Italian coffee bars offer variations on a typical cappuccino: a *cappuccino chiaro* has less coffee and more milk; a *cappuccino scuro* has more coffee and less milk. If you prefer to drink your coffee in a glass instead of a cup, try asking for a *caffè al vetro.* And if you need a truly eye-opening wallop, order a *caffè corretto,* a shot of espresso spiked with grappa or another liqueur.

Cafés form one of the great features of Parisian life.
. . . Most of the Parisian men spend their evenings
at the cafés, where they partake of coffee, liqueurs,
and beer, meet their friends, read the newspapers,
or play billiards or cards.

—*Baedeker's Paris and Its Environs,* 1907